GW01099483

THE LAWS OF GOLF

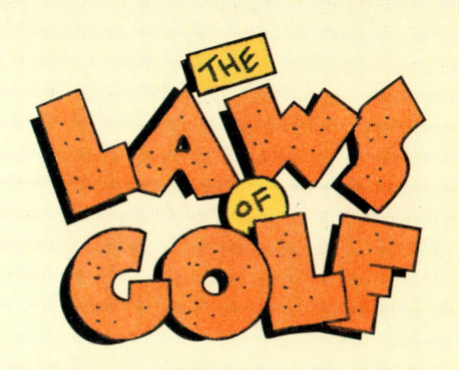

RANDY VOORHEES

A Mountain Lion Book

Andrews McMeel Publishing

Kansas City

THE LAWS OF GOLF

copyright © 2001 by Mountain Lion, Inc.
All rights reserved. Printed in China. No part
of this book may be used or reproduced
in any manner whatsoever without written
permission except in the case of reprints
in the context of reviews. For information,
write Andrews McMeel Publishing,
an Andrews McMeel Universal company,
4520 Main Street, Kansas City, Missouri 64111.

ISBN: 0-7407-1459-7

Library of Congress Catalog Card Number:
00-106923

Book design by Holly Camerlinck
Illustrations by Elwood H. Smith

INTRODUCTION

Golf is like a teenage love affair: exhilaration one minute, utter frustration the next. Mankind has invented no tougher game to master.

At first blush golf seems little more than a simple stick-and-ball game: You take your stick and whack a motionless ball toward a stationary target. How hard can that be?

But you don't have just one stick, you have fourteen, each of which is a different length with a different loft, and most often, each of the fourteen clubs has a manifestly different track record with you as its partner.

Moreover, the ball doesn't just lie there unprotected on a flat surface, waiting for you to pulverize it. Nooooooo, that would be too easy. Instead, you are confronted and confounded by uphill, downhill, and sidehill lies. The ball bounces left when you wish it to bounce right; it dives into ankle-high grass, and it ignores your commands (Get up! Sit down!) and protestations (Oh, don't go in there!).

But there are days when things go right. The ball bounces off a tree into the fairway, or skips through the bunker onto the green, or hits the flagstick traveling at mach 2 speed and drops into the cup. And you hit enough good shots to make you think that maybe you've finally figured it all out. So how do you separate truth from fantasy?

Some golfers, mostly veterans who have endured every bad break the game has to offer, understand that luck and misfortune—the rub of the green, in golfer's parlance—are an inevitable part of the experience. These intrepid realists simply endure with equanimity what the golf gods dish out. They understand that if something bad can happen, it will.

However, the vast majority of golfers aren't similarly blessed with acceptance. These tortured souls still believe that they have control over their golf games, that their scores will be dictated by swing mechanics and course management. They don't understand that golf's higher authority will not allow perfection, so they continue to tilt at flagsticks. It is for these romantic, quixotic duffers that we present THE LAWS OF GOLF.

THE LAWS OF GOLF is a collection of immutable truths about the game; it is a reality check that will put golf into better perspective for those who ask

INTRODUCTION

the eternal question: "Why me?" And strictly for entertainment purposes, the pages have been sprinkled with a few devilish definitions that were inspired by the greatest cynic of them all, Ambrose Bierce.

The laws of golf are absolutes that govern all play; they supersede any rules, and there is no relief from them. They are to golf what Murphy's Law is to everyday life: Anything that can go wrong will go wrong. Once you understand that it's the laws, not bad luck, that determine your golfing destiny, you can stop whining about those bad breaks and increase your enjoyment of the game.

So remember, when you're lining up that crucial putt to win the match, there's a force greater than you that will decide the outcome. There, that ought to stop your knees from knocking.

The Laws of Golf 1

The ball in the fairway is your opponent's. The ball in the fairway bunker is your partner's. The ball in the footprint in the fairway bunker is yours.

• • •

It's bad form to pick up another golfer's ball before it stops rolling.

The club you hit best on the practice range will be the one club you never have an opportunity to play during your round.

• • •

{ **par, n.** A level of play manifestly inconsistent with one's abilities. }

The Laws of Golf   3

The longest holes will play into the wind and the shortest holes will play downwind.

4   The Laws of Golf

Your shank off the 1st tee will be witnessed by millions and your birdie on the 14th will be witnessed by one (including yourself).

The surest way to hit the ball into a hazard is to aim at it or away from it.

It never rains when you're three down with three to play.

• • •

If you think golfers don't really root for one another, wait until your boss is standing over an important three-foot putt.

• • •

If you think you can clear the water, you can. If you think you can't, you're right.

19th hole, n. *A place where golfers take shelter from thirst and are exposed to a fury of lies.*

• • •

Every time a friend makes a birdie, you die a little.

The Laws of Golf 7

It's only after you lose your power on the tee and your nerve on the green that you have time to play more golf.

If everyone agrees that the putt breaks right, it breaks left.

8   **The Laws of Golf**

It's easy to tell if a golfer is lying about his handicap. If his lips are moving, he's lying.

The wealthier your playing partners, the more they will cost you.

• • •

Golfers are living proof that practice does not make perfect.

golfer, n. *A person indistinguishable from a rodeo clown by his fashion and a snail by his pace.*

• • •

Want to hit the longest iron shot of your life? Try laying up short of a water hazard.

• • •

Having another golfer praise your swing is like having the executioner say you've got a pretty neck.

golf pro, n. One who preaches impossibly complex doctrine to men he knows to be idiots.

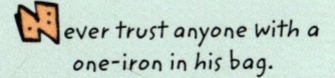

• • •

Never trust anyone with a one-iron in his bag.

Golfers burn incense before truth
and honesty, then grant each other
gimmes and mulligans.

• • •

Sometimes you have to hit
a second slice to really appreciate
the first.

• • •

There are no ugly swings,
only ineffective ones.

The Laws of Golf 13

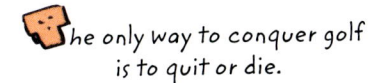

The only way to conquer golf is to quit or die.

bogey golf, n. *A lowly virtue whereby mediocrity achieves an inglorious success.*

• • •

There is no force so powerful as a shank whose time has come.

• • •

Golfers have been conditioned to revere newness, whatever it costs them.

The right to a second chance (i.e., mulligan) has deep roots in American culture.

There is no justice in golf, only tragedy.

You can't birdie the second with your mind still at the first.

• • •

No one holds their follow-through (poses) after a lousy shot.

• • •

lesson, n. Where the golf pro drafts a plan of your swing and plans a draft of your money.

The quickest way to ruin
your score is to accept
an invitation to play through.

• • •

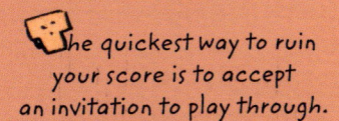

Never accept advice from
anyone who can't beat you.

The Laws of Golf

The surest way to play lousy on Sunday is to play well on Saturday.

Any golfer who says
"I can't play worse"
need only wait a few minutes
to prove himself wrong.

• • •

Everyone played better yesterday.

• • •

Ten-foot par putts are easy
when your opponent has
already made birdie.

Don't give putts "in the leather" to anyone using a long putter.

• • •

nassau, n. A betting contest in which the lesser of two liars enriches the other.

• • •

Equipment may change, but bad swings and bad scores remain.

The Laws of Golf 21

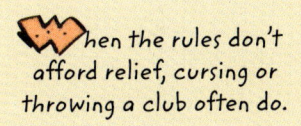

When the rules don't afford relief, cursing or throwing a club often do.

Living with a golfer is more grueling than being one.

One of the worst things
that can happen in life
is to play golf well
the first time you try.

• • •

The sandbagger's creed:
It is morally wrong to allow suckers
to keep their money.

• • •

Every golfer has swing advice
in him, which is an excellent
place for it.

The Laws of Golf 23

The brain is a marvelous organ;
it starts the moment you wake up
and doesn't stop until you get
to the 1st tee.

The best way to guarantee a 300-yard drive is to say, "This is a provisional ball" before swinging.

• • •

yips, n. The outward manifestation of an inward fear.

There is nothing so fragile
as a good swing.

• • •

Talk is cheap until you
step onto the lesson tee.

• • •

We are drawn to the 1st tee
in much the same way
we are drawn to the scene
of an accident.

Your short game is like a campfire: It disappears if unattended.

The surest way to mis-club is to pace off the yardage to the hole.

Golfers do not conspire
to circumvent the rules;
they just ignore them.

• • •

{ **golf cart, n.** A vehicle
big enough to carry two in
good times but only one in bad. }

• • •

Hope is that feeling that
deserts you just before the
long par-3 over water.

To travel the world playing golf is to discover that you can stink on any continent.

• • •

If a round of golf were a fish, most would be thrown back.

A well-dressed golfer isn't.

• • •

There is no cure
for the common yips.

• • •

God made the earth,
but it took a masochist
to invent the pot bunker.

caddie, n. An ingenious device by which golfers may escape individual responsibility for poor play.

• • •

A new driver won't make you a better player, but you have to buy a lot of new drivers to figure that out.

The more a golfer talks about the rules, the faster you should hide your wallet.

One benefit of playing with better golfers is that you can usually drag them down to your level.

Golfers who think they know everything are very irritating to those of us who do.

• • •

The first shank is like a lemming.

In the long run, titanium is cheaper than lessons.

• • •

foot wedge, n. An instrument employed in the rectification of golf course boundaries.

34 — The Laws of Golf

Start every round off with a smile and get it over with.

Fairways are a lot wider than greens, so if you can't hit the former, don't expect to hit the latter.

• • •

The bunker rakes are strategically positioned to stop your opponent's ball from reaching the sand.

• • •

They call it "rough" for good reason.

The little acorn is
a loose impediment;
the mighty oak tree is not.

The odds of making a
hole in one are roughly the same
as finding Tiger Woods's wallet
lying in the parking lot.

sandbagger, n. One who picks pockets with his tongue.

• • •

The best way to impart backspin on your ball is to ask someone else to hit it.

• • •

Never play with anyone who doesn't know what a "snowman" is.

Never ride in a cart
with anyone wearing racing gloves.

• • •

No matter how slowly you play,
the group in front will
always play slower.

• • •

Repair all pitch marks, unless
they're located in your opponent's
putting line.

Allow faster golfers to play through, then hit into them on the next hole. As a courtesy, be sure to yell "Fore!" when you do.

• • •

gamesmanship, n. A gift that is better to give than receive.

• • •

It is bad form to yell "Get down!" while your opponent's ball is over a lake.

Gravity does not exist in that area extending from the surface of a putting green upward into infinity. This is in stark contrast to the area over water hazards and cavernous sand bunkers, where the gravitational force is ten times greater than anywhere else on the planet.

There need only be one leaf on the ground to invoke the "leaf rule."

• • •

Golf balls and fairways possess like charges and therefore repel one another.

Looking into another golfer's bag
is as perilous as peering over
a man's shoulder while he's looking
into his wallet.

• • •

gimme putt, n. The beginning
and end of quid pro quo.

• • •

If your conscience won't allow you
to kick a ball from the rough onto the
fairway, then have your caddie do it.

The Laws of Golf 43

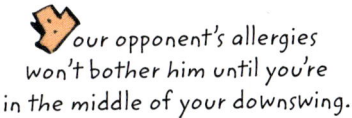

Your opponent's allergies won't bother him until you're in the middle of your downswing.

You are not entitled to line-of-sight relief from the woods.

• • •

You may not declare your opponent's ball unplayable.

• • •

It is as easy to recover from Bermuda rough as it is from the ebola virus.

The Laws of Golf   45

The better-looking the beer cart attendant, the more expensive the refreshments.

If you remove the flagstick, the ball will roll over the hole. If you leave the flagstick in, the ball will deflect off the green.

The deleterious effect of wind on golf scores is indisputable and may be quantified using a simple mathematical equation. Multiply the wind velocity (WV) by 2. The product is the number of additional strokes (AS) added to your score (2WV = AS). Therefore, if you normally post a score of 74 (ha ha!), a ten mile-per-hour wind will increase your score by 20 strokes to 94. It is important to remember this law of golf when explaining a suspiciously high score to the handicap committee.

The theory of ammunition states that the number of balls lost (BL) during a single round is equal to the number of balls in your possession (BP) at the beginning of the round.
Thus, BL = BP.

Even under optimum conditions (no wind, no one standing on your right, etc.), a perfectly struck slice cannot fall to earth more than ten yards behind the spot from where it was launched.

• • •

The only trees that are "90 percent air" are those located adjacent to out-of-bounds areas.

No scientific evidence exists proving that golf balls are intelligent life forms. Even supposing golf balls had minds, their solid exterior coating would prohibit shouts of "Get up," "Get down," and "Kick left" from reaching any hearing mechanism located within the interior of the ball.

Clubs thrown downwind will travel further than clubs thrown against the wind.

• • •

The velocity of a speeding golf ball (miles per hour) divided by 100 is equal to the height (in inches) of the welt raised on the body of the golfer it strikes (V$\beta \div$ 100 = HW). Therefore, a two-iron shot traveling at 120 miles per hour as it impacts the body of a golfer will raise a welt exactly 1.2 inches in height.

The Laws of Golf   51

There are three things in nature that are never downwind: a smoky campfire, raw sewage, and a short par-5.

There is nothing like a forced carry over water to prove that déjà vu is a bonafide psychic phenomenon.

For a golf swing, the ideal ratio of shoulder turn to hip turn is 2:1. This position can be achieved by exactly one person on the planet, including Tiger Woods.

The Laws of Golf 53

A stimpmeter is a device used to measure the speed of greens. A ball is placed on a grooved bar that is raised until the ball rolls free. The distance the ball rolls is measured in feet, then that distance is said to be the "speed" of the green. To obtain consistent results this testing is done on the most level section of the green, on the exact spot where you will never encounter the flagstick, so the stimpmeter helps golfers know the exact speed of the green in a location where they will never be putting.

1st tee, n. The death of endeavor and the birth of disgust.

• • •

Titanium is a hard, corrosion-resistant metal used by golf equipment manufacturers to make clubs that will enable golfers to hit the ball farther. Instead of your drives landing only five yards into the woods, they'll land 20 yards into the woods, and because titanium is also used to make lighter shafts, you will add significant yardage to the distance you can throw a club.

The area of a circle—with one exception—is equal to the radius squared multiplied by π (3.1416). The circular golf hole is the exception. The area of a golf hole is equal to one-half the diameter of a golf ball, except when your opponent is putting, in which case it is equal to twice the diameter of a manhole.

Symbiosis is defined as "the living together of two dissimilar organisms, especially when mutually beneficial." In nature there exists the case of the rhinoceros and the yellow tickbird. The tickbird feasts on parasites that infest the rhino's skin. The tickbird eats and the rhino doesn't have to scratch himself so much—it's a symbiotic relationship.

The Laws of Golf

In golf we have the case of the golfer and the beer cart attendant, the attractive young person who drives a bar on wheels. The golfer, frustrated and tension-ridden because of his poor play, ponies up big money to be soothed and refreshed by the cart attendant's offerings. The golfer gets an attitude adjustment and the cart attendant gets money.

golf lawyer, n. One skilled in circumvention of the rules.

• • •

Taking relief does not mean finding a bush and relieving yourself.

• • •

A birdie putt grows in length each time the story is told.

The Laws of Golf — 59

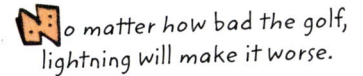

No matter how bad the golf, lightning will make it worse.

The divorce rate is double the norm among couples who golf together.

• • •

The best way to find a lost putter is to buy a new one.

• • •

forged irons, n.
Knockoff clubs.

People who live near golf courses
always hate golfers.

• • •

Balata balls will help you
play better the same way
a logoed shirt will.

Nobody ever asks about your score unless they know their score is better.

The six words every golfer hates to hear: "Your swing looks so beautiful today."

The Laws of Golf 63

Golfers root for one another
the way beauty contestants do.

• • •

There is no greater joy
than watching the club champion
miss a three-footer
for all the money.

Never accuse anyone of cheating who can run faster than you.

• • •

hacker, n. A member of a large and powerful tribe whose influence in golf has always been the enrichment of others.

• • •

All golfers ridicule other golfers' swings, mostly behind their backs.

The better you become at golf, the more you will be sought after by the golfers who used to snub you.

• • •

cellular phone, n. An invention that revokes all the advantages of leaving the office for the golf course.

A rich duffer has no enemies.

• • •

Nothing reveals age as quickly as a short, downhill putt.

• • •

The size of a golfer can be measured by the size of the thing that makes him angry.

You can't get to heaven if you don't count every stroke.

• • •

Hope for the best, but hit a provisional ball just in case.

• • •

When investing in new club technology, remember that nothing is invented and perfected at the same time.

golf, n. A game with much law and little justice.